T0146418

Awakening to
GRACE

Dharma Joy Penketh

BALBOA.
PRESS
A DIVISION OF HAY HOUSE

Balboa Press books may be ordered through booksellers or by contacting:

Balboa Press
A Division of Hay House
1663 Liberty Drive
Bloomington, IN 47403
www.balboapress.com.au
1 (877) 407-4847

Because of the dynamic nature of the Internet, any web addresses or
links contained in this book may have changed since publication and
may no longer be valid. The views expressed in this work are solely those
of the author and do not necessarily reflect the views of the publisher,
and the publisher hereby disclaims any responsibility for them.

The author of this book does not dispense medical advice or prescribe the use
of any technique as a form of treatment for physical, emotional, or medical
problems without the advice of a physician, either directly or indirectly. The
intent of the author is only to offer information of a general nature to help
you in your quest for emotional and spiritual well-being. In the event you use
any of the information in this book for yourself, which is your constitutional
right, the author and the publisher assume no responsibility for your actions.

Any people depicted in stock imagery provided by Thinkstock are
models, and such images are being used for illustrative purposes only.
Certain stock imagery © Thinkstock.

Print information available on the last page.

ISBN: 978-1-5043-0537-2 (sc)
ISBN: 978-1-5043-0538-9 (e)

Balboa Press rev. date: 12/01/2016

Publishing information

What I write in this book on various topics is purely my experience of them at the time I went through the training or the experience. It is not a specific or even general authoritative text on events or institutions, it is purely what I have chosen to convey about my own experience, and in my own words, other than quotes. Names have been changed to respect the privacy of some people. There are a few real names that I have sort and received permission to use.

Sam'skrta words are used freely in this book. There is also a glossary of terms at the back of the book. Pronunciation of sam'skrta words: vowels are a = ar (as in: far), e = a or ay (as in: display), i = ee (as in: knee), o = oh (as in: open), u=oo (as in: luna). m'= ng (as in: sung), a - at the end of a word is often silent, krt sounds like it has an 'i' in it, hence sam'skrta is pronounced sungskrit. Please look up the glossary at the end of the book for pronunciations and meanings of words and terms.

I swim in the Ocean of Your Unbounded Love.
Your Grace is Everything. I am Yours.

Tubhyameva Samarpayet Ba'ba'

"Life will give you whatever experience is most helpful for the evolution of your consciousness."

~Eckhart Tolle

Contents

"**Awakening to Grace**" is a stand-alone book that is the first book in a series called "Spiritual Coach: Spiritual Teacher". It is about experiences that have been significant in my life and that I hold tremendous gratitude for. This little book is all about Grace.

Introduction

Whether we are aware of it or not, the whole of life is about Grace. That we exist at all is purely Grace.

Our scientists have yet to find out why we exist. They don't know how we exist. They have fields of knowledge as to what exists, and how to research and manipulate it. They have investigated the tiniest particles and considered the vastness of space, and their knowledge is still far from complete. They just don't seem to know what it is that created this life, what animates it, what runs the system, and why life exists at all. What to speak of consciousness? Indeed, there is very little understanding of what actually consciousness is. What is it that engages us in this dance of life?

Grace is not something that can be examined in a science laboratory, or a psych lab. Nor even can it be experienced in philosophical discussion. I remember when I had the stunning experience of compassion, which in itself was an experience of Grace. I was about forty-two. Before this epiphany experience, I had studied and randomly read about compassion, so I had an academic appreciation of it. When I actually experienced it, it was way beyond anything

I had entertained in my mind. Experiencing compassion this way was definitely an 'inner' experience.

When I have experienced extraordinary Grace it is never the same. I recognise this Grace because of the energy coming with it, or the energy that is it. You will start to recognise by now the limitation of words in attempting to describe and explain it. It is just not possible. Perhaps poets, particularly those who specialise in the spiritual field come close to it. When I talk about Grace in the following chapters of this book, what I am doing is reliving it and writing it down descriptively as I go.

I do not know the 'mechanisms' of Grace. I don't know how life is put together. I think that must be one stunning mind-blowing story. What I have is my own relationship with the Divine. My heart and soul story. It feels like I am in the ultimate and most profound romance. It is a deeply evolving awareness of the sweetness of that Grace, all around me. Writing this book has been wonderful, and in itself, Grace.

My wish in writing this book is that it benefits you in some way. Even though I have written it as 'my' story it really is part of the human story. It is a love story, and it belongs to all of us.

As you will see as you read further, I have lived and worked as a spiritual teacher. I have also worked as a yoga teacher, an art teacher, a communication skills teacher and a qigong teacher. Now I work as a spiritual coach. My overall mission for the last two years has been working towards establishing a spiritual women's ashram in New Zealand. 'I' will do the work, and the flow of it and the outcome is all Grace.

1

My Early Life

Meeting Glimpses of my Eternal Self

"The initiation of the awakening process is an act of Grace."

~Eckhart Tolle

My Eternal Self is my Soul.

My Soul is part of the Greater Soul. In essence they are the same. When the individual soul unites with the Divine Soul that is true yoga. This is the real goal of human existence. This is the truth.

On the spiritual path, the Soul is also on its journey of expansion. The mind expands, becoming more and more subtle, expanded and open. The physical body becomes more subtle, refined and efficient. Attachments to the world; the world of physicalities, of beliefs and ideas, of addictions and unconsciousness eventually drop away as you surrender your constructed identity back to that from which you have come.

There is we are told, but a thin veil between living in ignorance (life after life) and living in truth. The effort required by us individually to go beyond this veil in order to attain enlightenment can be immense, and can take a number of lifetimes of intense inner focus and selfless service to come to that awakening.

Awakening, self-realization and enlightenment are the same thing: the profound expansion even beyond our wondrously expanded minds, to our own consciousness merging into that Divine Consciousness. This is the spiritual awakening.

Of course there is another awakening that is on the verge of happening right now. Humanity needs to wake up to the Political-Religious-Societal dogmas controlling us now in the 'global' arena. Insights and awakenings here will be in the realizations that humanity is one. Take away our various programed limiting beliefs, and we will see others as no different to ourselves and we would wish others the very best in life. We would appreciate then the world we live in for the unique expression of the spark of consciousness in all.

Our parents are here to give us, as a soul, a physical body, as an entry into the world of form. The physical body we have chosen to inhabit, is our vehicle, our little space ship, within which we navigate our life experiences. The body is a gift and precious. Without it the soul, on earth, does not advance or develop.

When soul makes its presence known to me it is like a 'truth' rises up in me. Something profound floods my being and I know something special and extraordinary is expressing itself. It is definitely Grace.

During my childhood in this lifetime my father was

a teacher, and for the greater part of her working life my mother was a school librarian.

Although I had memories from about the age of four, it wasn't until I was almost six that I had my first standout memory. That's when I became aware I had a mind that could interpret the world through written words. I clearly remember writing this two sentence poem and being so excited to discover I had a brain that could string words together. I remember when I had created this flow of words, rushing to find my mother and telling her about my remarkable achievement. Today over fifty years later I can remember the utter wonder of using words to express a concept of mind. Of looking into myself and using words to describe it. So here's that fantastic poem:

"Cowboys shoot guns at the Indians.
The Indians shoot arrows at the Cowboys."

Before you laugh too hard, note that this is a very perceptive social commentary that is still highly relevant today. It explains semi haiku fashion that duality exists, that action is a natural state of existence, that using power over others always brings a reciprocal energy, that imperialists exist, that your life and lifestyle can be usurped, that human beings are intent on killing each other (mostly under order or threat), that more than one sub-culture exists (the main culture is that of human culture), that strong stereo-typing exists, brain-washing exists, and that if you want to change the state of affairs you need to do or be something different. There is so much knowing that you could suppose from this six year olds poem and her first recognition of mind.

I was not brought up in a spiritual or religious family. Neither were they atheists. On one occasion, when I was nine years old, I was playing outside one summer day. My mother was hanging out the family washing. Out of the blue I asked her, "Mum, what is God?" She stopped what she was doing and went into a kind of reverie. She then said, straight out of a stillness, "God is love". So simple. I felt the energy of it immediately resonate deep inside my consciousness, and my insides seemed to wake up to it, like a switch had been turned on.

I used to be a 'Girl's Brigade' member. They are like Girl Guides, and after attending Girl's Brigade one late afternoon I was walking up our long drive and then path to home. It was now dark and I had turned to walk up the steep hill backwards. To distract myself from the darkness around me I was looking at the night sky when the thought came to me… 'what is there at the end of the universe?' I had an inner image of the physical universe just coming to a stop, and then there was nothing. Just an emptiness. What was the emptiness? For my ten year old self that was a really huge question. I knew in that moment that there was more. It was an answerable question. Right then, it was so big that I took fright and ran as fast as I could the rest of the way home. When my mother saw me she asked if I had seen a ghost, I looked so white. I just knew that that had been a powerful existential thought.

When I was thirteen, I was in the 4th form (10th grade). I was late into art class this particular day because of a prior arrangement. All the students had been given a small ball of clay to work with. As soon as I had mine I set to work immediately. In my spontaneous creation I sculpted a nun kneeling, with her hands in surrender. I got some more clay and made a bigger sculpture of two nuns standing next to each other. I still have both of these sculptures. The other kids in the class had all made pinch pots. I hadn't heard the teacher's original instructions. Perhaps I was late, yet perfectly on time in order to sculpt the nuns? Was this an inspiration or message from my soul? I cannot recall thinking about nuns before.

My father and I did not have a close relationship. He was emotionally unavailable and I responded to that. Yet on this one occasion I was so inspired by my thoughts, that I shared them with him. He was doing some building work in front of the garage. I said to him I was not going to call myself Miss anymore, I was going to be Ms. He laughed at me and said fancy his daughter calling herself 'Manuscript Penketh!' Then I said I had decided to be a priest, and that there was a seminary down in Christchurch I could go to. He laughed even harder and then after a while said angrily while shaking his pointed finger at me, 'no daughter of mine is ever going to stand up and preach!' I was shocked by his responses. I felt it as a wound going straight inside. In my moment of inspiration, I had enthusiastically and somewhat naively shared with him two very significant things to me. The feminist understandings and the fledgling spiritual orientation were to become life-long themes for me. I'd forgotten in the moment about his habitual putdowns. At this time, I was fifteen. Since that time, I can acknowledge that I remember my feminist and sanyasi stirrings at this age because of my father's standout response. That's the silver lining.

After completing college, I went to art school at

Canterbury University in Christchurch. I was still sixteen. I knew I was going to study art, because nothing else seemed to stand out to me or my parents regarding my vocation. Spirituality was not part of the curriculum, so it would have to be art.

At university I made friends with two other students called Christine and Amy. We were at Christine's parents place one evening with another of her friends and they decided to do a séance. They set up the Ouija board in the lounge. I chose not to join them. It didn't feel like it was something I was to do. So I sat in the room on the floor, with my knees to my chest watching them. What I am going to say next is not about possession, which you may think especially related to the Ouija board. It is completely different. After some time, I realised something was happening to me. My head was moving up and back until I was lying down on the floor. I felt amazing. I was fully absorbed in this experience. After a while I could hear the people in the room. Christine had got her mother and they were shouting at me to wake up, and trying to get me to take painkillers and generally panicking around me. I couldn't talk for a long time. They wanted to call the doctor, but I was almost completely gone in this experience. After a while they got me standing and walked me home, which was quite a distance. They got me to hold the carrier of the bike, even talking of tying my hand to it so they wouldn't lose me. I was in a state of bliss all the way home and into the next day.

In retrospect, I think what happened to me was to stop the Ouija board experiment from going ahead. I later found out that Ouija boards are definitely not recommended and have had some awful consequences.

During my years studying art and painting I was also intent on searching for something that made some kind of sense to me spiritually. I knew it was in the spiritual direction because my searches led me towards yoga, meditation groups, churches. I asked my tutors what was life about? What were we really? Where is here? and what was the purpose in being here? Tell me who I really am! I had about a ten minute interview with an orange robed visiting swami called Swami Gitananda. Nobody was able to give me any answer that resonated with the truth I was seeking. My peers at art school tolerated my frequent out-loud questions as to why we were here and who are we? "Uh oh, here she comes again!"

In my second year at art school I spent the Christmas holidays with my aunt and uncle and cousins in Tasmania. I had taken a book with me called The Fourth Way by PD Ouspensky on Georges Gurdjieff's teachings. It seemed a dense book and I was slowly making my way through it. I came to something Gurdjieff said, about if you deeply, deeply want something you need to call out to the universe or the creator. I was very struck by this. I had been searching and searching for something with my whole being so if this would help I was prepared to give it a go. I had an opportunity not long after as I went bush-walking near Mt Wellington. No one seemed to be around, so feeling this desperation intensely inside me, I shouted out to the universe to please help me and show me the way I had to go, please! After that I felt better, more relaxed. So now I was on the look-out for the answer. I was eighteen.

While this searching behaviour was the main inner feature of my life other things had been happening as well. For example, I started and stopped drinking coffee when I was thirteen. I couldn't stand the effect the caffeine had on my energy. I never ever drank it after this. I was offered a glass of beer after I'd finished mowing the lawn on a hot summers day. I never had any alcohol after this. About the same time, I had pulled my mattress off the bed and was sleeping on it on the floor, to my parent's dismay. It just felt normal to me. And at seventeen I became vegetarian, and have been since. First I gave up meat, then onions, eggs and fish. This was while I was living in my family of meat eaters. My mother, forward thinking as she was, bought me my own saucepan. No dead animal vibe in that.

When I consider all those events I have mentioned, some perceptive person might have said to me, either you were a monk or nun in a previous life, or the universe is clearly preparing you to be one in this life. Or perhaps both. I recognise that I carry a strong spiritual warrior or monastic archetype, which is sometimes more to the fore than at other times.

Eliciting insight.

Start out by using your breath to slow your mind to go into a calm and still place. From this place consider the following questions.

Your Early Life

Think of your early childhood (1-12 years):

1. Recall the powerful experiences you had at this time. Make a list.
2. What information was each experience offering you?
3. What was their underlying message?
4. How was this applicable in your life then?
5. How are they applicable in your life now?
6. How can you use this message to make the greatest difference on your spiritual journey now?
7. What is it you need to do to integrate this learning into your life now?

Do this exercise also for your teen years, and your young adult experiences.

Can you discern from the results of this exercise what your core pattern is? The one triggered early on in your life for you, curtesy of your parents, siblings, caregivers, peers and society. Knowing your core pattern is a true gift. Work out the platinum lining and then as the insights rush in let the chaff of your old memories go.

2

Spiritual Training

Meeting a new way of life

Initiation

When I returned to New Zealand, I spent a week with my parents in my home town of Nelson, before returning to Christchurch and study. On my first day back I was in town and happened to glance at a bookshop window and there was a poster advertising a talk by a spiritual teacher on the "War of Dharma". I was riveted! I took note of the details of time, date and venue. My friend wouldn't go with me, so I went alone. The teacher was an acarya of Ananda Marga. He wore an orange top and turban and a white lungi (long wrap around skirt). He had long hair that looked a bit like he had ringlets and a beautiful face and smile. He looked just like he was out of a Botticelli painting. I found out later that he originated from the north of Italy. His name was Dada Kashyapa. I can't remember the content of the talk. I do remember this incredible wash of energy coming through me and knowing immediately that this is what I was to be. My request to the Cosmos had been answered. I knew without a doubt I had found what I was seeking. Now I was on an even more determined path.

Sometime later I came to understand that what I was actually looking for was already inside me, inside my own existential "I" feeling. What I had found was indicators toward that knowledge. Which was fantastic.

The next day I went to where he was staying in order to learn meditation. A number of people were living there and I remember waiting for Dada for nearly two hours. When he did come out to the kitchen where I was waiting for him, he asked me what type of meditation did I want to learn? Universal mantra? Nama mantra? or Is'ta mantra? I had no idea what any of those were, but because Is'ta sounded like he had said Easter, and it was a familiar word, I said Easter mantra.

After a short time, I was sitting on the floor in front of him in the lounge, learning meditation. The door to the lounge had been left open. I had never meditated in my life before. I had a stunning experience. When he took me through the initiation process something powerful happened. In retrospect I know that my kundalini was awakened through the force of the Guru during initiation. I sat absorbed in the most incredible state for about an hour before the teacher called to me and I reluctantly returned. I felt light and expanded and bright and amazing inside. Blissful.

Not long after, I met other teachers who came to New Zealand. An American Dada, whom I had the pleasure of meeting again recently after about 40 years. He has set up healing centres in many parts of the world. Back then, I organised talks for him.

A version of the brilliant Universal Mantra Meditation

This is a tool to calm and still the mind. It gives your mind a positive focus. Your ability to meditate improves with practice. Your mind becomes subtle and expanded. It regenerates you. It increases your personal power, your confidence. It connects you with the Eternal Divine within.

To meditate, set time aside daily, ideally before breakfast and before dinner, about 15 to 30 minutes. Sit cross legged or on a chair with spine straight. R-e-l-a-x. Slow your breath. Already introduce thoughts of consciousness expanding within you. Witness stillness increasing. Notice an inner experience of expanding into the Divine, of being the Divine.

Gently continue to slow your breath, drawing more air in as you do. R-e-l-a-x. Listen with your inner ear carefully. Take your mind and your vision out to the horizon. Take it past the walls of the house, the trees and hills, way out to the horizon. Like you have x-ray vision. Calm your vision. Find the 'still point' out there. Now, bring that still point slowly back towards you. Draw it into the point between your eyebrows. Your eyelids will gently and naturally close. Bring the point of stillness into the centre of your head. R-e-l-a-x. Mind is still and deeply relaxed.

Now, as you breathe into this still point allow your mind to gently say the words 'baba nam' and on the out breath the words 'kevalam'. Your calm inner ideation on the meaning is most important. It means Divine Love is Everything. Fill the still point up with this love.

When your mind, resting in the still point in your head,

repeats the mantra, and the ideation of it echo's after, the mind is engaged in something highly positive and therefore liberating. When you finish meditating, just notice the corners of your mouth gently lift, the light of love in your eyes and the feeling of gratitude in your heart.

Spiritual Training in Sydney

Soon I found myself leaving art school, with one topic incomplete (I finished my degree much later). Now I wanted to learn about the world of spirituality. I was intensely focused on it. My whole Being seemed to be racing towards it. I went to the introductory teacher training in Sydney and for three months meditated, did yoga asanas and took the basic introductory classes in spiritual and social philosophy and yoga psychology. We were also during this time asked to get part time jobs to help support ourselves while there. The experience was powerful. From that time, I have a connection still with others who were also there even though we were in our late teens then and are in our 60's now.

After this training I was offered a place to work in the main office in Sydney. I worked on the magazine they published. I also used to do the food shopping for everyone at the office at the early morning markets. I really enjoyed my experience, particularly living with spiritually oriented people. One of the unusual standout experiences I had there was when I had returned back to the office after finishing a karate self-defence class and went to do my noon time meditation in the meditation room at the front of the house. Everyone else had done theirs and already had lunch, so I was meditating alone.

I did some kiirtan and then sat to meditate. I wasn't long into it when I felt my body being lifted off the ground and moved. I was surprised and shocked all at once. I put my feet down on the ground – I had been sitting in padmasana pose – and said out loud for 'it' to stop and put me down. I looked around and couldn't see anyone or anything there. I went to the door and left the room. As I went into the office one of the workers saw me and asked me if I was okay. He said that I looked white as a sheet. I explained what had happened, and everyone went into the meditation room to check it out. The meditation room had no furniture in it, so there weren't any regular places for the thing to hide. We looked outside too just in case the "thing", the energy was out there!

We all did Kiirtan again and sat down for meditation. Shortly after, one by one everyone left, leaving me alone in the room. I meditated. Then suddenly there it was. I was lifted up again off the floor pushed forward and then turned and pushed into the door. I had to push myself back hard in order to open the door to get out of the room. All the time telling 'it' that it was okay, I was leaving. By now I was shaking a bit and I ended up doing my sadhana in my room. It never happened again and I can't explain it. I was about 19 at this time.

I was now in the flow of going to train to be an acarya, a spiritual teacher. This is what I had been looking for all my young life. I made a brief visit home to New Zealand to sell my van and to thank my parents for raising me and to tell them what I was going to do. Then I left for Sweden where the training centre was. I lived and studied there for one very intense year.

Further Spiritual Training – Sweden

A typical day in training comprised: up at 4.30am, dip bath, dress, tidy bedding, kiirtan (singing to align one's vibration with a sweet consciousness), sadhana (focused meditation), collective kaoshikii nrtya (a women's dance for optimum health and spiritual well-being), and asanas (yoga exercises). It was all done in silence - moanabrata (silence with cosmic ideation) - except for the singing of kiirtan. Then everyone undertook their morning duties, then a collective breakfast, clean and tidy up in time for the arrival of the trainer for morning class. After this, we did kirtan again, sadhana and had lunch. After duties we studied in silence. Then there was break time and we would just relax, go for a walk, or just rest. Then duties again before akhanda kiirtan in the later afternoon for three hours, followed by sadhana, collective kaoshikii nrtya, and evening asanas. We would have a light meal, do more study, then late evening sadhana and bed after 10pm.

I had many experiences in training. During the three hour kiirtan one day I sat down to meditate and did not remember anything else until I became conscious. I was lying down in the meditation room. It was dark. Everyone else was asleep. I felt a little disoriented. Next morning, I asked what had happened. They said I had sat down to meditate, slid sideways and they couldn't 'wake' me, but in all other respects I was fine, I was breathing and alive so they straightened me out and made me comfortable. I was out about 5 or 6 hours. The interesting thing is that the next morning I felt amazingly refreshed and clear in my energy, even more than I would feel from a good nights' sleep. My co-trainees thought I was clashed (upset) about something and I needed to deal with it and this was one of the ways. I know now I was unconscious. My teacher says that when one is in a coma, unconscious karmic stuff can be 'burnt' and disappear. When one wakes, their life is often very different. I had the sense that things had changed for me internally.

In training I was the scribe or note-taker of the trainers talks that he gave after weekly collective meditation. Then he asked me to make them and the news from the training centre into a training centre newsletter. I did this and enjoyed the work. I have to say here that all the 'sisters' lived in their own house and the 'brothers' lived in their own house some distance from each other. All classes were given separately. Our trainer was a monk and he lived at the brother's house, only visiting us to give classes, and for collective meditation once a week. Then one day we had a visit from a nun of Ananda Marga. She stayed with us a week and it was very interesting to hear her stories of working in her postings. This nun was also a feminist and as such our discussions seem to get even deeper. I need to add here that one of the specific duties of teachers of Ananda Marga is the upliftment of women on this earth. This is because when that happens all of society will be uplifted.

One day we were having a discussion and the trainer arrived at the house and as he walked into the room I could feel and see this energy around him as he moved passed me into the room. I could almost touch it. It really stood out. It was very different to the strong yet subtle energy the 'sisters' had been generating in the room. This trainer acarya was a tall, slim Indian who wore all orange – turban, top jacket, and lungi (to the ground skirt-like wrap around) – and I saw him as a genuinely good and elevated person. I was curious about noticing the extreme difference in the female and male energies.

So as you can see, my young life, just like many other young people have experienced, had its share of significant events that shaped my inner and outer life.

Eliciting Insight

Start out by using your breath to slow your mind to go into a calm and still place. From this place consider the following questions.

Your SHeros Journey – finding your soul path, the path with heart and integrity. For this process you really need to allow yourself to imagine and envision.

Consider this:

Your parent's (caregivers) home is your nest of childhood. It is also your launch pad from where you launch out into the world and from where you discover your world. ***Consider your launch pad. What does this say about you? What does it say about your environment?***

When you hear the inner or outer call to action, gather what you need as resources, including your own inner resourcefulness, and take the first step. ***In what form did your call come? What are these resources?***

You may spend time searching, re-searching and imagining. This is also a resource. ***What kind of search, re-search and imagining are you doing?***

Move in the direction you are being guided towards. Trust this is the direction. Do not over analyse. ***What is this direction?***

The time to act is now. Observe keenly your inner and outer environments as you go. Consider what you see, hear, and feel in relation to your own energy and life. What kind of action is being asked of you? ***Describe this action: what is it like? what is it for? What does it give you? Where does it take you?***

Going on this journey, you discover you meet someone who will become your ally. They have a specific role in your life. They have powers you greatly admire. Through your relationship with them you acquire powers unique to you. ***Who is this person? What is their role in your life? What powers do they bring to your journey? What do they want from you? What are they here to give you? What treasure, elixers or magic is found with their help?***

On your path you will come across hindrances and obstacles. You will need to battle against these both internally and in the external world. Perhaps a darkness that will bring up fear. Something that makes you stand up for yourself, that will make you stronger. ***What are the obstacles? What effect do they have on you? Do you let them defeat you? Or do you do whatever it takes in your power to overcome them? How do you get through this part of your journey?***

You discover a treasure. It is something special and real to you. It uplifts you, it makes you experience yourself as a valiant human. ***What is it you find? How does it enrich your life?***

You know it is time to return home now. You arrive

home with your 'treasure'. You realise it is to now benefit your community and all human kind. ***How is it being 'home' now? How does this treasure benefit others? What is your life like now?***

3

Guru

Meeting my Beloved

"The desire in your mind to meet God is only born when He is inclined towards you. It is the result of His desire to meet you. Your meeting with God is not a unilateral affair, it is a mutual thing. You walk one step towards Him and He will come twenty towards you."

~Shrii Shrii Anandamurti

I pass my first set of exams and other tests and became an acarya.

I find out I am to work in India, in Mumbai, although I was there when it was Bombay. I fly into Delhi and take the train to Calcutta where I do the last part of my study and am now fully qualified as an acarya. Then I go to Patna to meet my Guru, Shrii Shrii Anandamurti.

I have arrived in India at a time in its history that would later be considered one of its most infamous. Indira Gandhi was Prime Minister and she had declared a National state of emergency that lasted almost two years. She imprisoned 140,000 people whom she considered her enemies: political opponents, protesters, activists, religious people, teachers, academics and more. She arrested monks and nuns of Ananda Marga, as well as their Guru. He was kept imprisoned for over 5 years by her government. His illegal imprisonment was eventually overturned by the High Court of India. During the time of his imprisonment they, those working in the government's employ, poisoned him. This had a long term effect on his health, and after that he refused to take solid foods and would only take half a cup of liquid yoghurt curd twice a day given directly to him by his devotees, until they released him from jail.

I'm mentioning this to you because I arrived in India to my posting just as The Emergency was lifted. You could say it was like the whole of India felt like it had been released from jail. I heard many stories from those who had suffered from brutal treatments. I also heard many stories of powerfully positive experiences. I remember one-day walking across a railway bridge in Mumbai when I heard someone calling out to me. I turned around and saw a young bright and shining Buddhist monk running to catch up with me. He introduced himself and said he had been imprisoned with some Ananda Marga monks and he just wanted to tell me how wonderful it had been to have been with them in their cell. He said it was like being in a monastery and in an energy of spiritual training the whole time. On another occasion one Ananda Marga monk told me being imprisoned had been a 'God-given' opportunity to do intensive meditation. The parents in the family I was staying with in Mumbai had also been put in prison. The women told me being in jail was a hoot. After you got over the shock of being arrested and settled in, she said she just got into preparing food for the other women in the prison with a cheery and compassionate energy. They even fed the jailers. She said the opportunity to do real service there was marvellous. There were so many amazing stories like that. I think that knowing their beloved Guru was in jail, made it easier for them to endure their own situation.

It is just like Victor Frankle said in his book 'Man's search for Meaning', "Everything can be taken from a man [or woman] but one thing: the last of the human freedoms – to choose one's attitude in any given set of circumstances, to choose one's own way."

After completion of my brahmacarya training in Calcutta and a visit to the training centre in Varanasi, I am permitted to go to Patna where my Guru is still in jail, to visit him. Another nun (Didi) and I are staying in the Ananda Marga office there a week waiting for permission to visit him. We have a message from Ba'ba' (the name devotees call him) through his personal assistant. We were to learn the specific protocol for meeting the guru and we were to be more controlled as regards to our laughing. We were really not meant to laugh out loud. It was pure excitement and all the feelings that go with that in meeting your Guru for the first time. Eventually I got to see Him. He was in a large cell with guards at the door. He was lying on a 'cot', a wooden bed. I think a fan was going. Three of us saw him that visit. A monk (Dada) who was a teacher in an Ananda Marga school in the south of India. A nun from Sweden and myself. Ba'ba' talked to each of us. He asked the monk how was his health, how were the children at the school? and said for him to take certain foods for his digestive problems. I noticed the sweet energy Ba'ba' had to this monk. Then Ba'ba' talked briefly to the Swedish Nun and she started crying. It wasn't anything bad, just the emotional intensity of the situation. Then he indicated for me to come closer to him. I did, and he said to me that men and women are like the wings of a bird. A bird cannot fly with only one wing. That men and women together comprise mankind. He said something else too that directly related to my thinking and experience in the Swedish training center, that I had kept private. My immediate thought on hearing Ba'ba's words was 'Who told you that?' No one could have. I had not yet understood that a Guru of Ba'ba's calibre could easily know this information, could read it in me, could know it from the ether and knew ones' past, present and future. This was his way of letting me know this.

I visited Ba'ba' four times while he was in jail. Three of those times were with the Didi from Sweden. On the second visit I was the one who was crying. I couldn't seem to stop. Ba'ba' talked a lot to Didi. While I was crying, I noticed what Ba'ba' looked like up close and the clothes he was wearing. He had a pale purple singlet, the type that has a hole pattern throughout it, and a white lungi. His teeth, fingers and feet seemed to me to be long and slim. I think that was an effect of his years of fasting.

On our third and last visit Didi was nearest to Ba'ba', as we were kneeling on the floor at the side of Ba'ba's cot, and I was directly opposite his feet. Didi was talking cheerily to Ba'ba'. Baba was propped up on his pillows and leaning on an elbow as he spoke and listened to Didi and asked her questions. So I was sitting silently at his feet when suddenly I feel this force pulling or pushing me forward and I could see it was taking me to his feet. I only had seconds to separate my hands on his feet as my forehead came down gently and slowly on the foot that was uppermost in his crossed leg position.

I stayed there in a deep and complete surrender and connection to my beloved Guru for what seemed a long time. Slowly when it (the energy) was finished I lifted my head and did a deep namaskar, then in this still intense energy I turned to look at Ba'ba' and was surprised to see him looking directly at me. When our eyes met I was just all open heart and soul and we were so still in a moment of what seemed like eternity, my eyes just fixed on his. That's when I noticed that it was so silent in the cell.

For the longest time after that I was in a deep stillness. I knew my life was changed. Something deep had moved and shifted.

Then there was something that happened in the very last visit that was somewhat mortifying, a tad embarrassing and quite funny, at least to me now. I had gone to the local markets to get a garland of flowers to give to Baba. I looked and looked. As I had finally decided on one, I heard my name being called out through the throng of people in the market. I couldn't see anyone. It was an older women's sharp voice. It was a bit of an eerie experience. I bought the garland, and in the afternoon I was able to give it to Ba'ba'. I don't recall who was with me at that time. The next day the news came that Ba'ba' had said, does he not pay his workers enough that they can only afford the smallest garlands. I knew he was talking about me! I felt embarrassed because I knew it was me, and wonderful and delighted that he was saying it at the same time! Maybe that voice in the market calling me was trying to tell me not to get that garland, but to get one that was from my heart and not my head.

Baba had a strict policy of not being alone with his female devotees. So when they went to see him they were always with someone else. Some of the male devotees had no such challenge. I also came to understand how clever Baba was in giving female devotees individual time with him while still maintaining his regular proper conduct. On the occasions I visited Baba in jail I was always with another Didi. I noticed that Didi cried on one visit and I on the other, so Ba'ba' was able to talk to us personally without the other hearing. That happened twice. Very clever and very loving of him.

I went to my posting in Mumbai. The head Dada there often went to visit Ba'ba' to report on work in the area. He would ask me if I had a message for Ba'ba'. So there developed a series of messages going back and forth between Ba'ba' and myself via this dada. It was a stunning experience. I found it was a bit of a struggle to adjust my western mind to Indian culture. I experienced lots of clash. It can sometimes be very uncomfortable while your mind is on a journey of expansion. Even though it was a challenge, the Ananda Margiis I met there were incredibly kind to me. They were wonderful. And even at the age of twenty-one, I could appreciate their efforts, their practical generosity of spirit towards me.

When I first learnt meditation, I was hearing lots of non-english words. I was intrigued more than put off. I came to understand that these words were sam'skrta, which I think is possibly the oldest language in the world. It's alphabet and words arose out of deep meditation eons ago by realized souls. They were created to vibrationally align with the cakra system. It is a highly spiritual language. When I first heard the word guru over 45 years ago, it was brand new to me. I hadn't heard it anywhere else in the world. So I didn't have any cultural overlay on it. What I did have was a sponge-like mind. Sam'skrta felt very familiar to me.

Eliciting Insight

Start out by using your breath to slow your mind to go into a calm and still place. From this place consider the following questions.

1. Who has been the most significant person, whether alive or historic who has had a spiritual 'impact' in your life?
2. What is your story about this relationship?
3. At what age and stage did they enter your life?
4. What was their influence and what were the qualities they brought with them?
5. What was your journey with them?
6. How does it continue to affect your life still?
7. What are you most grateful for in your relationship with this person?
8. How do you share the transformative gifts you received with the world now?

4

Spiritual Teacher

Meeting Grace

Denmark

When I completed my training in Sweden, I travelled with the Trainer and another new Didi and Dada to Denmark. While we were there we visited an Ananda Marga vegetarian restaurant that also ran free soup kitchens regularly. We were there in the early part of the day, so they were not open and the people who worked there were telling us how they ran it. Suddenly there was a loud pounding on the door and someone went to open it and this very angry, dark energied man came in. No one could understand what he was saying, but we could all understand and feel the raging energy coming from him. Everyone seemed transfixed by this startling intrusion. From where I was standing I just started to say the universal mantra of Ananda Marga, which is 'baba nam kevalam', which means essentially that 'everything is that supreme consciousness'. My volume when saying it increased as I moved slowly towards the man. He was still angry and turned to vent it on me, as I got close enough he spat at me. I just continued to stand there repeating the mantra out loud. Then suddenly he stopped and turned and left, slamming the door behind him. Everyone seemed to breathe a collective sigh of relief. It had been a potentially volatile situation. Now it was over, and after a while we left. We did discuss that he may have been demanding food, or something else. Even so, he had been incredibly angry and intimidating. I don't know if he went back again. They would have helped him if he had.

While in Denmark I gave my very first initiation. A woman approached me asking to learn meditation. She was a young doctor from Iran.

Germany

We continued our journey to Germany and to the training centre located there. During the time I was staying there I was to experience three things that have stayed clear in my memory. The first was when a young man approached me and said he was having problems with his devotional feeling. As a new acarya, I said to him what had helped me, and that was, in a private moment calling out to that Divine Consciousness with the sincerity of your whole heart, and with powerful intent to be shown the way to devotion. That evening we heard someone shouting loudly in the huge field of maize at the back of the training centre. Of course it was in the German language and when I asked for a translation was told he was calling out to God for help with his devotion. Wow. I think he thought he had some privacy deep in the huge corn field. His words were probably crystal clear for miles around. It would have been interesting to know the impact he had on others who heard. I think it could have been spiritually provocative. It could have resonated with some deep soul part of them that was on the edge of awakening. As Anandamayi Ma says: "To cry out to Him is never in vain".

The second story is when another young man came up to Didi and I with the titles of two talks, one for each of us to present. Didi immediately took the one on devotion and I was left with a very academic talk on some aspect of spirituality I was not very familiar with. Needless to say Didi's talk was a resounding success and mine was, well… not. The margiis there were clear in their evaluation of the talk and very disappointed. Not the best start to talks as a new Didi.

The third event happened when we went for an excursion into a nearby city. While others went to purchase food and other things in the shops I walked on further into the city. Then something happened. An energy seemed to be pulling me towards this huge square concrete building on a corner of the street. I stopped and stood still, amazed. As I looked at this unattractive, serviceable building, I felt my heart expand, and I was filled with love. I felt love pouring out of me and coming towards me from the area of the building. I had a clear and distinct feeling of having lived there before. It felt like coming home. Where that building was I knew I had been loved. Very deeply loved, and I had loved in return. It was like I was in some kind of trance or altered reality. I stood there for a long time just feeling this love. Then the others came to get me to say it was time to go back. The feeling of that love stayed fresh with me for a long time.

We travelled on to our retreat destination in Rome. It was held in a beautiful, very old and large monastery with arched walkways and colonnades, and vast rooms. The architecture of the buildings and the beautiful landscaping were stunning to experience. We were there a week. Then I flew out to India.

Thailand

After India, where I lived and worked for about a year, I was posted to Thailand. I stayed with a woman there briefly, and then very suddenly the time came when I had to look for another place immediately. I knew my situation could get dire by the evening. I was new to Bangkok, so I really had no idea of what I should do in this potentially difficult situation. Yet I felt very calm. I knew Ba'ba' would come up with something. I was not asking. I was just surrendering myself and the circumstances.

Before doing anything further that day I needed to get a visa issue sorted and I had taken the public bus to the government offices. In Thailand buses have seats at the front of the bus that face the driver. I was sitting about half way down the bus looking out the window. I think the bus was near empty and it had slowed down to a crawl because of the traffic, when this man got on the bus and sat not quite opposite the driver. He turned and faced me. I couldn't believe it. It was Ba'ba'. I was so amazed that I remember checking for indications that it was actually him. Yes, they were all there. The glasses, his clean shaven face, his hair style, his shape and size, his clothing style, including his shoes. I could hardly believe it. The convincer for me was his pearl ring. It was on his finger and he was touching and turning it with his other hand, almost as if he was deliberately drawing my attention to it. As soon as I fully realised that it really was Ba'ba', the bus slowed to turn the corner and Ba'ba' calmly stepped down and walked off into the crowd. I sat there just dazed. It was a very strange and wonderful experience. I knew Ba'ba' was in India and Bangkok at the same time.

Immediately after this my circumstances changed. I found the passport office. The man helping me asked what was my current address. I said I had just left the place I was at and was not sure where I would be tonight. I was very calm and quietly positive, even when I knew I was 'homeless'. The man said to me, "My uncle is a retired Thai air force colonel and he has a big property just outside Bangkok with a separate building. Let me call him and ask if you can stay there". So he went away and some minutes later was back with an affirmative response. This was wonderful. I was amazed at how my guru was looking after me. The man drew a map and gave me all the contacts and directed me to a bus that goes past that house. He even wrote in Thai a note for the bus driver to drop me off at the house. When I met the Colonel, he was a lovely elderly man who spoke excellent English. There were a number of other family members living there. He was a very gracious host and we had a number of interesting conversations about life and spirituality over the time I stayed at his place.

As part of my posting I worked in Malaysia, Singapore and the Philippines. While in the Philippines I decided to go on a 'mono-diet' of milk powder, water and papaya for six weeks. It was wonderful. A clean out for the body, mind and spirit.

Phillipines

While in the Philippines I travelled the islands and visited the training centre in Davoa. The trainer there introduced me to a newly qualified Didi. She was originally from Indonesia. I talked with her for a while, but even before that I could just feel the most beautiful energy radiating out from her. It was an uplifting experience just to be in her presence.

Even though I was still relatively new to the field, I was posted as Didi-in-charge in South East Asia. My friend from training in Sweden had been in that posting before me. Not long before I arrived Didi had self-immolated in a public park in Manila. I was shocked. In the training centre in Sweden Didi and I had been close and respectful friends. I was challenged by her decision, yet what could I do but accept it also. I don't know the details of this vast Cosmic Play, so the best I could do was be respectful of Didi's actions and just surrender my inner experience.

Back in Manila, the Dada who was head of Ananda Marga there started to order me to see him at his office at least once a week where he would very angrily tell me off for not controlling my workers. What he was talking about was another Didi in Manila who had started a children's school, written and published books, raised funds for medical projects in the Manila slum areas, and many other projects. In short, she was a dynamo of energy, capability and networking. I thought perhaps he was jealous of her ability and didn't realise it.

When a person becomes an acarya, they do so with all their human robustness and frailties. Meditating 4 times a day, doing yoga asanas twice a day, and dry fasting four times a month, for years, slowly changes a person. It is like one is on the way to becoming a divine human. On this journey tricky things can still come up in the mind such as anger, jealousy, and acting out, depending on one's reactive momenta. I noticed often that my Guru would put one into direct scenarios where these can be brought to light and given the opportunity to be worked with and surrendered. The ego can often make these, particularly negative mental occupations, excruciatingly painful to let go of. Ego fights hard to retain them because these are among the ways it keeps us in unconsciousness.

So I experienced a problem with this Dada's unawareness of his anger. I really did not know what to do. I asked other teachers for help. No one would or could. So I felt alone in my situation, and that was familiar to my ego. However, something mysterious happened. One day an internal voice started to talk to me. It wasn't my inner-talk voice. It was a very different sort of voice. It was a lovely voice. Very easy to listen to. I wasn't sure it was male or female, but thought perhaps it was more male. It was telling me some kind of story. I never thought to write it down. It told me this story without stop all day and all night, no matter what I was doing, meditation, asanas, talking with others, eating, sleeping. It started, from memory on the Friday, and finished the moment I got off the jeepney to go to our collective meditation, on Sunday. I did feel a bit disconcerted when it stopped because I had gotten used to it and I felt its loss. It had been so beautiful to listen to.

When we went into the meditation place, which was at that time a very large dojo, there were about 150 people present. We sang the 'baba nam kevalam' kiirtan and did collective meditation. After we came to the end, a young man stood up and said my name, and that I would be giving a talk on 'The Importance of the Guru on the Spiritual Path'. Wow, I was very surprised to hear that. No one had mentioned that to me. The English Didi sitting next to me nudged me and said "You never told me you were giving a talk. I never saw you do any research or specific meditation for it". I said to her, as I was starting to stand, that it was alright. I went up to the front and asked the young man if he had a microphone, whiteboard and pen. He said he didn't. I said that's okay and turned to face my audience. I closed my eyes briefly, remembered my guru mantra and started. I recall the talk lasting about 45 minutes. There was no stumbling along the way. It was just a wonderful flow of inspiring words, all the words I'd been hearing for the past two and a half days. Purely by Grace they had been given to me and purely by Grace they just flowed from me. The Margiis clapped at the end. Usually they don't do that and then I went to my place to sit again. Even Didi was saying, "Wow, that was amazing!" It was a very different talk to the one I had given in Germany! The demonstration of that was clearly His Grace too.

It later became clear that the in-charge Dada had tried his best to set me up. He wasn't there at that collective meditation. He had wanted to embarrass me for some reason. But something amazing had happened. I was saved from this potential humiliation by the intervention of my Guru.

A short time after this, almost on an impulse, I left being a teacher. That Dada also left. I heard later he had come to find me to apologise. We had both been players in His Divine Play.

Not long after I left, a curious thing happened to me. For the following three weeks I was in an energy field like a cork screw made of light. In my whole body, from head to feet, from my whole being, I felt the sweetest most sublime energy, leaving me. I knew what was happening and I felt a tremendous pain that Ba'ba' was taking the acarya energy out of me, and at the same time He was doing it with such tenderness and I felt such bliss that I could do nothing but be with it and surrender. It is His Grace to give and take. I have already seen how He blesses and bestows in other ways. I am just truly grateful I had the experience of being His worker and living as a sannyasii.

I will say here that this time ranks as the saddest and most poignant in my life, even beyond the heart wrenching death and loss of family members and friends. I cried a silent and sometimes not so silent ocean of tears. In my mind and in my heart I pleaded with Him to not let me go. For about five years after that I felt like I was hanging off a spiritual cliff by my finger tips and it was purely His Grace that I did not fall.

Some years later I came across this quote of Anandamayi Ma's: "Once the Guru has accepted a disciple, He will never leave her until the goal has been attained. The question of leaving does not arise at all". I felt tremendous relief and gratitude on reading it.

Enough of this seemingly sad part of the story. Looking at the whole of it one can also clearly see the exceptional blessings in it. We are all His actors on this Life Stage. I think we are mostly sleep walking actors, playing parts unconsciously, without any knowledge of the big cosmic picture. We just need to do our parts to the best of our ability, and surrender the outcome. Even more, we need to wake up. How amazing this life, this world, would be if we all made the effort to spiritually awaken!

Eliciting Insight

Start out by using your breath to slow your mind to go into a calm and still place. From this place consider the following questions.

1. **Experiencing awe and wonder at the Intensity of Grace**: Grace is being poured down upon us every minute of every day. It does not have to have the light, sparks and colour of the animator's imagination. But it is there. The very fact we have a life at this time is Grace. Having a life where you take the opportunity to meditate, to uplift yourself and others, where you follow a life of Dharma is tremendous Grace.
   Have you ever been conscious of experiencing Grace?
   What form did Grace take?
   How did you feel about it?
2. **Guidance:** Recall a time when you experienced guidance that was beyond the capacity of your own thinking or the advice of others.
   What was that experience?

What was the guidance?

Where do you think it came from?

What did it show you?

What was your greatest learning from this experience?

3. **Profound Loss:**

Have you experienced something precious leaving you?

What was that?

What was it like?

Why did that happen?

What did you learn from this experience?

How are you using that learning in your life now?

4. **Acceptance:**

Did you reach a state of clear and open acceptance regarding the loss?

Even a state of gratitude that you were given it in the first place?

And gratitude that you noticed the blessing in its loss?

Did you reach the insight that something so profound may come again, at any time?

What was that like?

5

A Counsellor

Meeting Compassion

This is just a very short story, that I remember clearly because of the lesson I learned and the stunning experience I had. One of my children had had a bit of a personal difficulty. At the time I was studying psychotherapy and thought I could find a counsellor to help. As it was, my child in the first visit, had a major problem with this counsellor, and told me the situation. So I made a time to see the counsellor to tell him what my child has told me about his behaviour and attitude in this first session.

When I met with him, he was very annoyed that I had showed up. He just wanted to do the session with my child. His behaviour towards me was obnoxious. I asked him to hear me out and when I started to speak his shock at being 'found out' and addressed made him instantly contrite and apologetic. His energy seemed to fold in on itself and somehow sucked him down right there in front of me. Then as I continued to speak to him a very peculiar energy seemed to come out of me, and surrounded me and filled my consciousness with an incredibly deep wave of compassion for this man. Any anger and sense of defensiveness I had against him, in regards to his treatment of my child just evaporated. I felt filled with an amazing type of love that just poured from my being. If I was being a bit fanciful about it I'd say it felt like a benediction for this man, and also curiously for myself. I could see him recognise what I was saying when I described the problem and he sort of flinched and couldn't look at me. When I finished he said okay, he would take this to supervision and let me know the outcome. As it was, in our next brief meeting he said he had changed his mind and his professional supervisor had said to him not to discuss anything with me about the supervision session regarding his unprofessional behaviour.

This was not an intellectual creation of a sense of compassion I experienced. This was the tremendous energy of compassion itself. Even though this happened twenty years ago, the energy of that compassion has stayed with me. Up until that time my understanding of compassion was as an academic and philosophical concept. I had never really experienced what it was.

Compassion is when no matter what you or I have done I feel a profound love and acceptance for you and your (our) humanity. It is like embracing the other in a state of unconditional love, and you cannot but be drenched in it yourself. Compassion fills the whole of me when it embraces the whole of you. Feeling compassion is a state of grace.

It is like becoming love itself.

This state of compassion, takes you out of the drama and directly into the loving openness of the human heart. It was a powerful and stunning experience.

The Dalai Lama's lifelong themes have been the emphasis on compassion and kindness. He has said: "A compassionate attitude helps you communicate more easily with your fellow human beings. As a result, you make more genuine friends and the atmosphere around you is more positive, which gives you greater inner strength. This inner strength helps you spontaneously concern yourself with others, instead of thinking only about yourself".

Eliciting Insight

Start out by using your breath to slow your mind to go into a calm and still place. From this place consider the following questions.

1. What is your story of finding compassion?
2. If you don't have it currently, look for the opportunity over the next month to create one in relation to someone you experience a challenging situation with?
3. What does compassion feel like to you?
4. What happens when you use compassion?

6

Communication

Meeting the Magic of Listening

One of the biggest reasons I found myself learning communications skills was that I realised my children and I were all different in our mind sets and styles of being ourselves in the world. It took me quite a long time to figure that out. I was so busy doing all the day to day parenting stuff, that at the end of the day I was utterly exhausted, so perceptive thinking and an intuitive flow were sometimes like a rare jewel. It was when I acknowledged to myself that my communication was not all ease and flow, that I was experiencing challenges handling their late childhood, and early teen years, that I knew I needed help in relating to them. I needed to learn the art and the science of a much more effective style of communication.

Initially I found learning the skills challenging. That's because the trainings at the beginning were quite dense in information. However as soon as the role plays kicked in that first day of training, I started to realise some amazing things and became a sponge absorbing all this new information

41

that I believed was going to help me make sense of my relationships, especially with my children.

Sometime after I did my last training in these skills, my daughter Jayanti, who was about fifteen at the time, came home from college, and as soon as she entered the house I could hear she was upset about something. But because I was in another part of the house and she didn't know where, she was shouting out the story of her upset and she sounded really angry about it. I had not long arrived home and I was sitting at the other end of the house from her. But when I opened my tired eyes I could see her coming down our very long hallway, heading for her room.

Something in me stirred and I heard the distress in her voice. I sat up and I knew immediately that if she went into her room I would have lost an opportunity to possibly change things around for her, and for me. I saw her reach for her bedroom door handle, so I said, at almost the same pitch and volume she had used, out loud the same thing she had last said. It had an instantaneous effect. Her hand suspended itself in mid-flight to the door handle, and without a pause, she said "yes", and continued her story. Next, she dropped her school bag at her door and turned towards me. I just said her last sentence back to her, just slightly modified so it didn't sound like I was copying her. She kept on with her story and started walking towards me. Her tone had changed. It was now normal voice volume. I kept reflecting the essence of what she was saying, back to her to let her know I was listening. Now she was in the room with me. It was like we were having a conversation, but it was her telling me about her problem, me listening and saying back to her what I had heard. Then unbelievably she perched herself on the arm of the sofa and the 'conversation' continued. Now she was starting to laugh. She was telling me the funny side of the same story. It was hilarious. We were having this really fully engaged, laugh-out-loud time. When she was finished sharing, she said, 'God, that was good Mum, thanks for listening'. We hugged, and my girl, now in a completely different frame of mind, left the room chuckling.

Later I told her about the reflective listening skill I had learnt at the communication training. She could see how I'd used it with her, and she said she hadn't noticed at the time. She thought it had worked like 'magic'. 'Thanks Mum'. Later, still impressed by the skills effectiveness, she said if I ever wanted to share that experience with people in my trainings, she was good with that, because it really worked. So with her permission, it is now in this book.

I appreciate how the Vietnamese Buddhist monk, Thich Nhat Hanh, says that when people are experiencing difficulties in their life, we could start by saying: "Dear friends, dear people, I know that you suffer a lot. I have not understood enough of your difficulties and suffering. It's not my intention to make you suffer more. It is opposite. So please tell me about your suffering, your difficulties. I'm eager to learn, to understand". He further says, "It has to start like that – loving speech. Then if you are honest, if you are true, they will open their heart and tell us. Then we practice compassionate deep listening. During this deep listening we can learn so much about our own perception".

Over the years of teaching and meditating, I have noticed I am not the only person on a spiritual path that has found communication skills invaluable.

Being drawn to the spiritual path does not mean you

automatically know how to talk to someone in order to resolve differences. Personal collisions can happen anywhere and if people are willing to learn and use effective communication skills, conflicts also get to be resolved in a really good way, at a deep level.

Eliciting Insight

Start out by using your breath to slow your mind to go into a calm and still place. From this place consider the following questions.

1. How many relationships have you stopped engaging in because you or the other experiences pain, and you feel too angry, or hurt, or humiliated, that you don't want to talk to them anymore?
2. How many families, couples, work environments, businesses, corporations, communities, towns, cities, countries also go to war because they don't have the will and the skills to resolve disagreements?
3. If you knew the specific skills in how to courageously speak and how to deeply listen, how would this change your life? What would be different? How would it change other's lives?
4. Research Communication Teachers in your area or who are able to teach you over skype. Choose the one for you. Start your new relationships journey now.

7

Spiritual Coach

Meeting Joy

"It is but the Self that calls to Itself, and none
other than the Self that realises Itself."

~Anandamayi Ma

I made a decision to train in life coaching in 2007 thinking
that I could easily transfer that knowledge to the spiritual
and vice versa. My actual intention was to become a spiritual
coach. Not long after I enrolled the training institute
started a spiritual coaching class and program. It was very
eye-opening for me. Even while I was new to this type of
work, with the help of the tutor and the group, I started to
hear and perceive things in new ways. As I listened online
to others coaching, I began to notice the level they were
coaching from, even from the very beginning of the session.
I understood too that a person's problem or challenge could
successfully be worked with on a number of levels: in the
purely practical external world way, through to the deeply

internal spiritual way. It very much depended on what the client wanted and how the coach coached.

It was an interesting process to find out what spiritual coaching was to me. Because this form of coaching was also new to my training institute, I noted that tutors and coaches who did not specialise in it would say that "everything is spiritual, therefore all coaching is spiritual coaching". Or "all coaching is spiritual coaching after the first three sessions". These may be a small part of it, but they so obviously had not worked as a purely spiritual coach. Spiritual Coaching in my experience is a very different approach, very different energy and a very different outcome for both coachee and coach, most especially for the coachee.

Before continuing I want to say that spiritual coaching is not religious coaching. Neither is it for me related to the New Age movement nor to psychics and psychic readings.

As a spiritual coach trainee, I remember one session in the training group where I was asked to be the coach. Up to that point I'd felt self-conscious about coaching in front of others because it was a new skill. Yet as soon as I was asked, in a split second I made a conscious decision and said yes and I felt all my energy inside shift to 'step up to the plate'. I was ready. The session commenced and immediately there was a 'clean' flow of energy between myself and the coachee. Some could say I moved into a leadership role, or that I had a particular confidence, or that I knew my stuff. Yet I knew it was something more. Through-out that session, and right up to the end, and for a week after it, I experienced an elevated inner energy. My mind was in an expanded state and in that time the world was very different for me. The session was amazing from start to finish. It was as if that energy took care of everything. On my part there seemed no effort to it.

Directly after the session when the tutor asked for my feedback, I struggled to respond to him. Even though I had been speaking during the session, my mind was in a very different flow or level in that session. It was like it had expanded out to relate and to lift the coachee at a 'spiritual level' and was now having to condense back to the intellectual and was struggling to respond to his academic questions. I'd have to say then that my coaching was clearly from my intuitive mind. Just to respond to his question which was now fully outside the session flow, it was even difficult just to say quietly and slowly, "I am sorry, I am having a challenge responding right now". My mind and my tongue were temporarily out of commission. For all that week after the session I was in a kind of bliss state. All the others listening in, including my student client, the tutor, the observers and the class also recognised something extraordinary had happened in that session.

Kenzie: A curious type of awakening

Prior to that experience I had been not so confident and experienced an inner struggle with my deep wish to work in this field, knowing that I had the ability in it, and not having the confidence to put myself out there as a spiritual coach. I found self-promotion a very tricky thing. Also at the beginning of my training I had not a clue how I would be as a spiritual coach. All I was really looking for was just to learn about my inner self and how that would manifest in my work.

Kenzie was a young woman with a master's degree. She worked as a yoga teacher in Boston, and became one of my peer coaches while we were in coaching training. She asked the question "What do I want from our sessions together'. I responded, "To know my true self and to be able to work from that place". Then she asked, "So, who or what is your true self?" Immediately I could feel my energy changing. Everything slowed down and I went into a deep, quiet and still place. For a while there I was not speaking or answering her question. After a short time, she asked me the question again, but I was not able to answer. I quietly asked her to please wait. I was definitely undergoing some kind of internal energy change. I just stayed with it and let it happen. I could hear her talking again, I struggled to find my voice, and I said to her, "something is happening inside, please wait. Give me space".

Perhaps if I had been able to think at that stage I would have said something like… 'I can't do this session. Something has happened. It feels amazing and important. I will get back to you for another time'. Or even to just hang up the phone and call her back with an explanation later. But I had no mind that could even think that. I was somewhere very deep and all I could do was to be present with that. So her questions continued. After a while I realised her questions were trying to pull me out of where I was and to put me back into my analytic mind. They were not helping me go deeper or even allowing me to stay in that space. So after a while every time she asked, I was saying "please let me be here…' or "please stop your questions…' "I am in a good space…' "please let me be here", "please stop, please, please", "stop the questions". In the end I actually started to cry in an aching desperation to go deeper into this space of moving into my 'true self'. "Please stop talking… I can't talk… please… please be quiet". When I realised fully that she couldn't hear me and just wait, or to just sit in silence for the session, I just said I have to go, and I quietly hung up. I just had to disengage.

That was the most powerful and the most tough session I have ever had in coaching. The power was in the question "So who or what is your inner self?" and then in going there. The tough was all the rest. Again that feeling of being deeply one with my True Self (I'm not sure how else to describe it) was so profound that the energy of the experience stayed with me for days.

A week later in the next session I attempted to explain to Kenzie what had occurred. I eventually realised she still wasn't able to understand. Even in the second session she was asking me questions from the academic perspective and energy, and not from the spiritual or intuitive one. I made an effort to work with her for a third time, since it was a training requirement to do twelve sessions. It was not possible.

That experience of coming to a new level of inner awareness, or a higher level of mind was something I have not forgotten. Ironically I think Kenzie in her unawareness and my somewhat distressed response to her intrusive, out of sync questions, has made it stand out even more as an important event. It also illustrates that just talking about spiritual things is not spiritual coaching. If Kenzie had had more awareness in this area the outcome could have been different, perhaps to the point of facilitating a deeper change in me. I later talked about this experience with a master coach who was a tutor with the coaching institute. That coach had a different energy and it was not possible for me to resurrect anew that experience of going deeper into myself. Seemed it could only happen with Coach Kenzie.

Lukas: Calling me Forth

I advertised and got another coach at the institute called Lukas. He is from Belgium originally and lives now with his family in the south of France. Lukas is a multi-talented person who among other things has been a mountain guide, an exhibiting artist, and is a business coach and an equestrian 'coach'. I was fortunate to be his client for a number of sessions, more than the twelve suggested by the training institute. After some sessions, Lukas said that he wanted me to coach him in the next session as a spiritual coach. Phew. I was a little nervous, but I said yes. So when that date came around I became the spiritual coach and Lukas was the client. As soon as I started coaching I could feel the energy change. We went through the session to completion, and at the end, in closing, I asked him how it was. There was silence. A very long silence. Then he said he couldn't talk right now he would see me at the next session, and we hung up. If the drama mind had been active at that point all sorts of negatives could have got in there regarding his response. But I felt a good energy, in the session and after the session. I felt calmly confident and so I waited the whole week till our next session, and in that session, Lukas told me that our session had been amazing for him. That the intuitive flow I was in as the coach had influenced his energy and he had felt himself elevated as a result and that had been an incredible experience for him. He said that the way I saw the things he had brought to the session to be worked on was powerful. He said I had pulled things together for him in a new way. I had helped him to create a new warp and weft in his life story that was incredibly healing for him. He also said he didn't mean to be rude last week by hanging up, it was just that he was in this very new place inside himself that he found he was unable and unwilling to speak to break the 'beautiful spell'. I have to say that what he was describing is also what I had been experiencing energy wise. I so appreciated working with this man. His being able to articulate and reflect back his experience of me, gave me, in turn, valuable insight into my coaching process and abilities. I realized what a gift insightful feedback is. Then there is this. I cannot claim the outcome Lukas experienced. I coached from some higher flow. It was not an ordinary everyday mind conversation. It was definitely some form of Grace.

The key to spiritual coaching is to
be still and present inside.

Mind becomes soft and expanded.

It is still, with nary a ripple.

You are present in your inner being-ness.

Everything else functions from this calm presence.

Being engaged with the other in the spiritual coaching
relationship is to be engaged from the intuitive mind.

All sensory perceptions, speaking, listening, feelings,
are all intuitively engaged. Analysis and intellect
take a back seat yet are also intuitively engaged.

The heart comes forward in a new way into the
soft and expanded mind, and then the vibrational
energy in the spiritual coaching relationship is
like a bright light as well as a healing balm.

Love is unspoken, yet ever present.

Eliciting Insight

Start out by using your breath to slow your mind to
go into a calm and still place. From this place consider the
following questions.

1. Recall a time when you have experienced a deep stillness
    inside. Feel that again now. Let everything relax without
    force or effort. Just be in that calm and still space. Stay
    there as long as you can or want.
2. Consider a relationship you have had where you had a
    truly uplifting experience and your inner world changed
    just like that.
3. Consider this: A'tmajina'na (art-ma-gee-arn), means self-
    knowledge. A'tma is soul. Jina'na is knowledge. Shrii Shrii
    Anandamurti says, "Self-knowledge is the true knowledge,
    and all other knowledges are the mere shadows of
    knowledge that do not give the exact idea of reality." Self-
    Knowledge is Self-Realization. So do whatever is required
    to attain Self-Knowledge. What will you do?

8

Zhineng Qigong

Meeting the Cosmic Energy

I had been involved with Zhineng Qigong in one way or another since 1999. I had been interested in going to China to study for a long time and a few years ago, I decided to attend a training with teachers in China. Deciding was such a process for me. To go or not to go? In the end, in my sadhana, I put the question (repeatedly) to my Guru "Am I to go?". The response would always come back a resounding "YES!" So in the end I went. I didn't know what to expect. I went with two women who had been my students. I had an amazing experience. The teachers there at the time were superb. They were all highly skilled and completely dedicated to their qigong practice and teaching. They all had a tremendous heartfelt respect for their teacher Pang Hee Ming. The students came from all over the world. If the time and circumstances were again aligned, I would go again in a flash. The qi field at the training centre, when you are in it is stunning.

In my visit there, something extraordinary happened

that was at the same time profound and rather beyond the scope of the training itself. In our third day there the formal classes started. We had arrived a day early and others were a day late. One of the teachers in the afternoon had just finished teaching his class. I was standing near the back of the training hall, so to leave the hall he needed to walk past me towards the exit. As he moved towards me a very curious thing happened. I became aware of an energy coming either out from my energy field or surrounding my energy field, encircling me. In my mind's eye I saw it was a dense, yet amazingly light filled circle of energy. Even in that very brief moment of time when this was happening, simultaneously my perception slowed down, awareness expanded, it felt as if I was witnessing it all with an intense focussed awareness, like I was participating in something I knew was meant to be happening, but I hadn't actually read the script.

I remember seeing subtle hints of intricate patterns in this energy field. The encircling light was a soft deep green, and very thick, about two thirds of a meter, and it seemed to reach out about one and a half meters from me all around. At the same time that this energy appeared to be flowing from me, it felt like it was filling me up. I knew it as an energy of 'loving recognition', or 'love' and 'recognition'.

As the teacher passed me, I was so stunned by this energy, that I actually turned to see if it was still there. It was. The energy just seemed to flow from and around me. It was linked somehow to the teacher. I was not sure if he had drawn it from me, or had in some way caused it to happen. Still in the moment, when I checked around the room, I noticed too it wasn't similarly connecting with anyone else in the training, and no one appeared to have noticed anything.

The energy stayed for the rest of the training. It was a very, very sweet energy. It was an open-hearted, genuine connection. Whatever it was it felt pure. Perhaps that was the real reason I was 'sent' to China. For this to happen. It was definitely a gift, and it was definitely Grace. Perhaps it was to heal a heart, or two? Perhaps we were to briefly meet in this life, for a reason only the 'Lords of Karma' know. Whatever it was, I was and am deeply grateful.

In relation to the reincarnation idea, perhaps there was some special connection in a previous life. When I asked the teachers where reincarnation fitted in with Zhineng Qigong they said the idea of reincarnation does not work for them. They think of something like my experience as a fortunate event.

During that training, a visiting teacher gave two formal evening talks. Local people who also did Zhineng Qigong attended too. The overall theme of these talks was about spiritual relationships. I found that very synchronistic.

The 'Blackness"

Also in that qigong training I experienced other things happening. The attitude of the teachers, with regards to paranormal abilities, having done this qigong for over 25 years, was to say do not get caught up in them or pursue them. So I will share just briefly bits of my experience. The head teacher had the ability to use a form of guided imagery that took you deep into the process he was teaching. In one session, my mind seemed to go. No thoughts, no senses doing their thing inside or outside my mind. I was very surprised by what then happened. My mind, I think it was my mind, expanded so far that it went into a nothingness. Inside everything seemed black. It was not a black of negative connotations, but a complete blackness of soft, restful, calm, in the all-encompassing expansiveness of inner space. It was to me absolutely beautiful. It felt like I was home. I stayed in this state for about two hours. After that session we had been told to rest. I think that is about integrating all the work. After I awoke, I found myself in my everyday consciousness again.

Mingmen

Another time, the woman teacher was teaching us the first method in in-depth detail. She was talking about how all the movements come from mingmen, which is located opposite the navel, at the back. In the evening I was doing my own practice of it in my room and I again experienced an altered state. Instead of using my mind to focus on the movements and the qi coming in, mind was not the main feature anymore. In a very sweet session I was aware of my body automatically going through the movements effortlessly without any energy expenditure or mind involvement. I watched inside me somehow and could literally see all the movements coming from mingmen. The qi seemed to be doing all these movements by itself. Yet mind calls and directs qi, so I would have to say it was a very subtle part of my mind that was doing that. 'I' was just a presence observing.

Skeleton

Another experience was when we were doing hip circles. The woman teacher was taking this class also. We actually did them for such a long time in one direction, that my legs were getting sore and on the verge of shaking from the effort. When she said we were nearly at the end, and then to centre the body, I was so relieved. Unfortunately, she then said to reverse directions and we did that direction for another twenty minutes. I surrendered my pain and closed my eyes, filling my legs up with qi. I focused inside and started to notice the qi accumulating inside my lower dantien (between navel and mingmen) area. As I was doing that, suddenly I found that I could see my skeleton from the inside. It was a bright almost glowing, luminous white, in a background of black. I was so surprised to see this that I looked with my inside eyes up towards my head and was even more surprised to notice that I saw the changing views of my skeleton as I changed direction. I was fascinated to see the skeletons movements as I was doing this exercise. As soon as we stopped the exercise, the visuals went.

Up until that time I never experienced these kind of phenomena in my own practice, so I think it was a result of my focusing consciousness and the powerful qi field the teachers were constantly building within every class. When I described my experience the teachers listened. Still, they reminded me the emphasis in practice was to cultivate qi for health, healing and vitality, not on phenomena.

"Pop"

Not long after I returned home from training, a friend called me about a friend of hers experiencing difficulty. She asked if I could help her. I met the woman at her house. I had met her before and knew she had experienced something similar a year before. I will refer to her as Dale. Dale was exhibiting symptoms of extreme stress. She seemed to be beating herself up. Her hands would hit her face and her chest, pinch her and pull her hair hard. She'd try to stop it but struggled to. As well, Dale made mewling noises and was exhausted. She was lying on the sofa. My intention was to get her to relax. I said for her to just allow her hands to do what they were doing and just to observe them. I said they quite likely had a good intention in doing what they were doing. After spending sometime reframing her symptomatic behaviours based on them having ultimately positive intentions, I got her to relax even more. I said for her to use her mind to draw energy into her body, into every cell. Her hands were still hitting her. Soon she fell asleep and as she was sleeping there was little movement. The ringing of the telephone woke her an hour later. During the call her hands started up again. She was actually trying to move her head away from them because the blows she was delivering herself were quite hard. I took her through relaxation again. After a while I said to her, I really didn't know what else to do. Did she have any ideas? She said she'd just have to tough it out because she didn't want to take the prescribed drugs again. I said I could ask my teachers in China for help. So I said their names out loud, said Dale's name and her current situation out loud and asked for their assistance. Suddenly in the room there was an enormous presence of total silence. Dale stopped all her hitting motions and noises completely and just lay there quiet and unmoving, for the first time in hours. In my mind I had felt something pop out of Dales navel just before the silence. I was stunned. Then Dale, lying quietly on the sofa, said something just popped out from her belly button. She said it was like a cork popping out of a wine bottle. She slowly sat up. We just looked at each other. Wow. Everything had changed just like that. Later I actually emailed my teachers and asked did they notice anything energy-wise at this time and date. They hadn't. I think in their world this type of experience is not unusual.

In this case I don't know what did the healing. I don't think I did any healing. I don't think Dale did the healing, otherwise she could have done it before I arrived. Perhaps it was that I said things that Dale's subconscious used to do her own healing. Perhaps some other energy had a part in it. I don't know. Definitely it was Grace that the situation she was in changed. The emphasis of Zhineng Qigong is to be your own healer.

There is something I want to add here that some will no doubt find provocative and others will immediately acknowledge. In his talk on 'Intuitional Practice and It's Necessity', Shrii Shrii Anandamurti says meditators develop superpowers. From my qigong training the trainers speak of it as developing paranormal abilities. These are also called occult powers. Healing using these powers may look and sound like magic, or right out of a science fiction or fantasy movie. Examples of this could be the 'pop' experience I had. Or it could be throwing psychic or chi fire down the throat of a person with throat cancer, burning the flesh, so you could smell it.

Disease and illness are the result of sam'skaras – reactions to past actions – and are a way to burn or pay for these karmic debts. All actions beget reactions. There is no way out of these reactions except to undergo them. If people use occult powers to heal another, they will themselves take on that persons sam'skara and will have to experience its effects. There are rare stories of guru's taking on the karma of their devotees to ease the devotees situation. That is never taken on lightly. If you are reading this book, I doubt you are a guru with the vast and profound knowledge of the intricacies of how karma works.

If a person heals another using occult powers, they stop this persons' self-development and spiritual enquiry. If you are well again at no bother to you, you just pick up your old rhythm of life again. Illness has two important functions: the first is to pay the karmic debt and the second is to provide a push and the motivation to heal their situation. During this time, new awakenings can happen at a remarkable frequency. At this time one can start exploring a spiritual path, or a form of natural healing. To learn meditation.

So how can a person then help someone heal themselves? The best ways are to teach them to heal themselves. People's healing paths are unique to themselves. There are so many forms and levels of natural healing: qigong, tai chi, massage, herbal remedies, homeopathics, yoga asanas, meditation, imagery, just using your mind in new ways, ayurveda, nutrient rich diet, exercise, laughter and much more. Then there is the science based medical care.

I recently heard about someone I know of in New Zealand who healed herself of kidney disease by doing qigong for a year. Instead of ending up on dialysis she was given the all clear. My Zhineng Qigong teachers in China told me about people healing themselves from pancreatic cancer, and many other diseases. I have read stories of people acknowledging that their experience of disease was the best thing that happened to them because in their search, efforts and determination to heal, they became stronger. They now engage in much more aware relationships and through it all created a richer inner life. This is by developing a healing state and frame of mind. Then through that, cultivating energy, stillness, focus, intention, and surrender.

Eliciting Insight

Start out by using your breath to slow your mind to go into a calm and still place. From this place consider the following questions.

1. Remember a time when you experienced another sense of reality. Perhaps you became aware of a different type of energy around or inside you. When you recall this experience consider its message.
2. Have you ever had the experience of taking your body and mind into an increased energy field, well beyond their ordinary level of energy? What happened? How did that feel? Did you continue to increase your energy? How could you do that even more?

9

Intuitive Group

Meeting Intuitive Alignment

I felt a really powerful need to connect more to my intuition.
I was talking to Zoe, an acquaintance, in town one day and
it turned out she ran a weekly group that was more to do
with readings, the psychic type, and included other things
like card reading, psychometry, prayers and that kind of
thing. I had never been involved with anything like this
before. My first introduction in the group was with photos.
Some friends of Zoe's were experiencing some difficulties
in their lives and had asked her for help. She brought along
to the group some photos of them and passed them around
Saying whatever information you get from them to record
it. I was squirming in my seat because I was new and this
seemed all very odd. When the photos came around the
circle to me I decided that I would pass them on really
quickly, a bit like a hot potato. When they did get to me,
even as I was passing them on, all this information came
flooding into me about them. I was stunned. I waited until
the download seemed to be finished. I went over to Zoe and

told her what had just happened. "Does this sound like the information you are wanting?" I asked. "Yes, it does."

As it happened, in that group I was able to develop a method of reading that was often spot on, though not always (although I did not feel it was my 'I' doing it). I remember being with Zoe and another person when she asked if it was okay to visit a woman who lived not far from her. This woman had asked her for help. I didn't know anything other than that. As soon as I got into the house I was getting impressions, and when we sat down with this woman they just rushed in. Zoe did a reading first. Then the other woman, and then me. I found it really hard to listen to what the others were saying because the impressions were still happening and I wasn't sure I could hold on to them while I waited my turn. I told her what my impressions and intuitions were and she sat quietly listening. When I finished she told us about her situation. It was about her husband dying, about work and more. I was surprised my reading had been so spot on. My words had come out clear, gentle and uplifting for her.

I had enough time in that group to appreciate the work of people with this type of intuitive ability. I was able to get in touch with a part of my own intuition in this way. I discovered different expressions of intuition and saw that we favour a particular type or style according to our sam'skaras. I also realised this was not quite the use of intuition that I was seeking.

I found again that I wanted my intuition to be in alignment and direct relationship with that Divine Consciousness. I wanted to focus my attention in that direction, and to so increase intuition to come to know what that Consciousness wants from me and for me at every moment, as I move in this world and beyond. The way to do that was to make every effort to move towards that Divine Consciousness in my sadhana. Sadhana after all, is an intuitional practice.

Shrii Shrii Anandamurti says that the Supreme "is beyond the range of your Buddhi (intellect), but within the range of your Bodhi (intuition)."

Eliciting Insight

Start out by using your breath to slow your mind to go into a calm and still place. From this place consider the following questions.

Consider a standout time where you recognised intuition was to the fore in your life.

1. What was this experience?
2. How would you describe your intuition?
3. How did you use your intuition?
4. What kind of inner space are you in when you use your intuition?
5. What do you consider the benefits of using intuition?

10

Tikanga Group

Meeting Rasa, the Divine Flow

About four or five years ago, there was a great divisive split in the group I was with at the time. Somewhat mirroring the rest of the world. Unbelievably it eventually led to a court case with winners and losers. What we have now are two groups of essentially good people, with extreme financial obligations, some have actually lost their homes, because they believed they were in the right and others were in the wrong.

In New Zealand at a retreat about 10 years ago, in an afternoon training presentation, I introduced a new concept based on the empowerment of the local people and suggested using 'Tikanga' as a descriptive name for it, as applied to our group. Tikanga (tee-kunga) is a Maori word that means many things: 'the correct way of doing things,' culture, lore, protocol, system and mechanism. Even though the training was well received, nothing immediately came of it. Still the seed had been planted. It was positive too, that at the time every person in that particular group (some of whom would eventually come into opposition) thought it was a great idea and a real solution to the divisions that were beginning to appear.

About five years after this something happened with the group in New Zealand. There was some secrecy around unilateral decisions being made on our behalf that we were unaware of, and that had the potential to affect everyone in the wider group detrimentally. When we became aware of this, seven people around the country and in Australia, independent of each other, challenged the so-called leaders of the group on their behaviours. We literally got no response. The seven of us eventually realised that there was a deliberate disconnect and we became deeply disturbed by what was happening. Between ourselves we started to discuss the situation. The energy was very heated about things, so it was easy to pick out themes right from the beginning.

I again introduced the idea of 'Tikanga' and we agreed to tentatively refer to ourselves as the Tikanga Group. It was easier than saying all our names, or the reason why we were together every time we wanted to arrange a meeting. For me Tikanga was a code that represented an empowered way of thinking and behaving that could make it possible to work with and eventually unite the divided factions in the group, especially when they were in New Zealand. It was perceived again as a positive and healthy solution.

As I said our Tikanga Group of seven were really upset about our perceived 'skull-duggery' of the others behaviours. At the beginning our meetings amongst ourselves were challenging. It seemed a lot of our personal stuff had to be sorted, and amazingly people were so fired up and committed that lots of this kind of work was moved through fairly fast. Then we got into how to conduct the meetings and what did we want to do about the situation. What was it we really wanted? Everyone in that group wanted the empowerment for the local New Zealand people in the group. An empowerment that in fact would also work for everyone, including those in apparent opposition.

If you are aware of the current world situation, you will recognise that what I am saying in this chapter echoes what is happening in the world. I don't think this is unusual. I would guess that many groups world-wide are affected by this energy. It feels very polarising. The thing is, if we can deal with it at the local level, then we know we can change it at an international level, through a new framework.

The Tikanga Group met on skype once a week. In some of those meetings the energy was utterly amazing. Transcendent could describe it. In one meeting in particular we were all openly working in a very focused way on what it was we really wanted that would work for all of us, based on the principles of Neo-humanism. It was while we were imagining that, that the energy palpably changed. It was suddenly very different in the room I was in at home where I was on the skype meeting. I could feel it, along with an overall sense of peace and wonder. There was a profound stillness, yet with an energy of loving upliftment. We were suddenly all very quiet on that skype call, becoming just present to the energy. All seven of us had gone silent. Eventually the person in Australia said into the long silence, "Do you feel that?" and in awed tones continued, "This must be His Rasa". Rasa means the flow of the Divine. It was utterly beautiful.

We noticed that this energy was there when the energies of our hearts and expanding minds were coming together more and were open to exploring positive change and inclusive ideas.

The other thing we noticed was even though we all lived in different places in New Zealand, and one was in Australia, this Rasa energy was felt by all of us. It did not matter where we were physically located on earth. So if the people of the world, no matter their location, their gender, or their work, came together with pure positive and powerful intention, and the outcome of that is surrendered, then from this experience I can say that something profound will occur.

One outcome for this group was that we all directed our energies to organise a meditation retreat together and most of us presented trainings based on the work of our Tikanga Group. Feedback from the wider group informed us that it was one outstanding retreat, with a great and meaningful focus that was clear and informative, inspiring, and truly uplifting. That would be Grace as well!

Eliciting Insight

Start out by using your breath to slow your mind to go into a calm and still place. From this place consider the following questions.

1. Think of a time you may have experienced in the past that may not have started well, where you may have been set for a 'show-down, and unfathomably it went in a very different and uplifting direction.
   - What was that situation?
   - What were you expecting to happen?

- What actually happened?
- What do you think contributed to the positive change in direction?
- How did you feel after?
- How did Grace play out in this?
- How did you know it was Grace?

11

Work

Meeting the Divine Play

A while ago I awoke from a deep sleep with something quite amazing running through my mind. I felt incredibly light, happy and excited. I quickly wrote it down. This is what I wrote:

> *"Another Glorious day in Earth School.*
> *Thank you, thank you, thank you.*
> *Who is the director? – Must be God!*
> *What stage am I on today?*
> *What will my lines be?*
> *What is the story?*
> *What is the general thrust of the energy?*
> *What is my role?*
> *What vibration do I want to carry in this role?*
> *Who will be on the stage with me?*
> *What roles will they be occupying?"*

Within about four hours of writing this, my whole life took a most radical and unexpected turn, in a way and to a degree that I have not experienced before. I had been in a surreal work situation for about two months already, hoping it would improve as I adjusted to my new role. This situation went from the wonderful, to a horror story very fast. Right from the beginning of this experience I recognised the hand of the Divine in it and I knew I had to release any control I might have thought I had.

That morning after I received the above 'message', I found myself witnessing the extreme end of the situation in which the Divine created a way for me to leave, that was irrevocable.

Part of me felt the stunning full body and mind impact of the experience. Another part of me was quietly enthralled and observing everything: me going through it, my behaviours, my energy and thoughts; the behaviours of others and from a curious birds-eye view I was watching the amazing orchestration of the whole series of inter-related scenarios.

Ultimately I was in such an extreme position that all I could do was to surrender. I knew right from when it started, that I had been given the above message as a perspective to hold as an actor, during the coming events. It was amazing. For some reason I was going to be in this intense situation and I recognised I had been given help via the message. Even when I woke up with the message I was curious as to how the day would unfold.

Afterwards, when the situation was over and completed, it took just a short time to recover and to integrate the energies and lessons from the experience. During this time, I recognised things were being rearranged internally. It was like I had come to the abrupt end of something big and now I seemed to be undergoing some elegant metamorphosis. Energies in the external world were changing too. The most immediate was my clear and decisive response to things. Intuition seemed to have speeded up, or rather my access and use of it had. This made my day to day experience fresher and brighter.

Eliciting Insight

Start out by using your breath to slow your mind to go into a calm and still place. From this place consider the following questions.

Part of the Play:

Recall over the past week, month or year, a single time when you have been with people in situations that you have not been in control of and things out of the ordinary have happened.

Now imagine in that situation that you are on a stage in a vast theatre. All the props look 'real' and people and things around you are not so unusual. Yet something has happened. The scene is being played out and you suddenly realize a degree of detachment to your own engagement in it. Then you get the clear sense you are an actor on this life stage. You realize there is nothing for it except to continue in character and say your lines, only this time with awareness and you watch the plot unfold or unravel. You just accept the exquisiteness of your awareness. You accept and surrender whatever your role and contribution.

What was the situation?

What were you aware of?

What did your awareness feel like?

What are your insights of the situation?

12

Reality Shifts

Meeting further new perceptions

Two years ago I was walking home after work. During the day I had briefly talked to someone about 'waking up'. It was an informative and inspiring exchange. It was 5.50pm and many people were on their way home from work. I turned the corner and looked up into the street and experienced a mind-reality shift. There in front of me for as far as I could see, I saw all the people walking towards me as asleep, as if they were human robots. I blinked to clear my vision but it stayed the same. I walked down the street quite stunned that I was being shown these people with their 'sleep' program turned on. When I got to the lights at the next corner I turned to look back down the street, just to check my perception, and sure enough I could still see the sleep walking people.

When I was a new mother to my third child, my daughter Jayanti, my partner and I were standing out the front of our home. He was holding our baby daughter and I was sweeping the front driveway. As I was sweeping I looked

73

up at Jai and suddenly she and my partner were literally giants towering above me. I felt really, really, small. It was like I was looking up to the height of skyscrapers. I looked down, closed my eyes and looked again…up really high. My partner, from his great height, said "It's not us, it's her. Jai's doing it". So he was aware of what was happening as well. It wasn't just in my mind. Jai's Maori name is Tumoana, meaning the crest of the wave. According to him, she was demonstrating the wave, a spiritual peak. A short time later things had adjusted back to what we consider normal every day perception.

Four years ago a young friend was experiencing what I would call a huge turning point in her life. We had a number of long conversations to help her steer herself through her challenges. At a certain point we came to a natural halt in this work together. Around the time it was drawing to a close she called me to share something exciting. She had been sitting in meditation and she said she was seeing a kind of movie of a beautiful lotus flower. She said she had never seen anything like it before.

I asked her the exact time and day this had happened. When she told me I was amazed. On that same day when I was meditating I had also seen a brief movie. It was of my Guru. It was like a snippet out of his day. He was talking to someone. I could hear the conversation, and as he was talking he turned around and sat down facing me. Then it finished. It was quite stunning.

Here my friend and I had done this work together and then simultaneously we both experienced a gift of Grace.

Eliciting Insight

Start out by using your breath to slow your mind to go into a calm and still place. From this place consider the following questions.

Recall, and if you are unable to do that, then imagine having an experience of a shift or noticeable change in your sense of reality or your everyday perceptions.

- What happened?
- What new understanding arose?
- How did you recognise this as Grace?
- How did this help you catch a glimpse of your True Nature?

End Piece

Being aware of the Grace we experience in our life is in itself extraordinary Grace. Part of the sweet mystique about Grace is that it mostly comes unasked. The awakening to Grace, whether through profound insight, a sudden opening of the heart, or a 'spiritual' experience, often comes through a period of deep inner communion, sometimes the result of a very challenging life event, or from the deepest yearning of your soul for something greater in your life. Or none of the above. Grace arrives in its own time and its own way and one's experience of it is very personal.

This little book is for you. It may be an odd little story to some and others will recognise themselves in it. Just know this. Grace is with you...all the time. With no exception. You... are already blessed.

Glossary

Acarya – spiritual teacher. One who teachers by example.

Ananda Marga – Path of Bliss. A social-spiritual organisation.

A'tman – Soul

Ba'ba' – Dearest one, most beloved. Feminine version is Ma or Amma. Devotees name for Guru.

Bodhi – intuition

Brahmacarya [bra-ma-chary-ar] – is a stage of training to become a spiritual teacher. Brahma is consciousness. Acarya is teacher. In this stage one learns that all is brahma and this is the example one sets in their teaching.

Buddhi – intellect

Coachee – is one who receives coaching from a coach. Coachee and client are synonymous.

Dada – monk, brother

Dharma – the essence of spirituality. Innate tendency that identifies something. The dharma of fire is to burn. The dharma of a glass is to contain. The dharma of a human being is to strive for and attain one's original nature. The path of righteousness in social affairs and conduct. The path of all humans that leads to enlightenment and liberation.

Didi [dee-dee] - nun, sister.

GOD – Generator, Operator, Destroyer.

Guru – spiritual preceptor. 'The "gu" of guru means "darkness", the spiritual darkness, the micro-psychic darkness, and "ru" means "dispelling personality". So Guru means "the personality who dispels darkness from the minds of spiritual aspirants'.

Is'ta [eesh-ta] – personal spiritual goal.

Karma – action.

Kiirtan [kee-er-tarn] – singing to align one's vibration with a sweet consciousness.

Lower Dantien – place to gather energy to, located between navel and mingmen. Other two Dantiens are in heart and head areas.

Sadhana [sar-dar-na] – focussed meditation; the effort for perfection.

Sam'skrta [sung-skrit] – ancient language from India based on sounds and vibrations of the cakras.

Sam'skara – reaction in potentiality. The reactions from past actions yet to be undergone.

Mantra [marn-tra] – word or phrase that expands and elevates the mind.

Moanabrata [moan-ar-brar-ta] – silence with cosmic ideation during the working hours of the day.

Mingmen – From qigong. Located opposite the navel, at the back.

Neo-humanism – is a worldview of love of the Divine Consciousness, and for all of creation, both animate and inanimate, as creations or expressions of the Divine.

Parama Purus'a – parama means great; purusha means consciousness. Infinite Entity. Supreme Consciousness. God.

SHero – originally in response to the 'Hero's Journey' concept of Joseph Campbell, and the inadequacy, bias and imbalance of the English language against women and favouring men. SHero is an inclusive idea of both the male and female.

Tikanga [tee-kunga] – a Maori word meaning the correct way of doing things. Protocol, system, culture, lore, mechanism.

Zhineng Qigong – 'Zhi' means wisdom and intelligence. 'Neng' means power or ability to heal. 'Qi' means energy and 'Gong' means cultivation. Using wisdom to cultivate energy giving the ability to heal body and mind.

References

"Life will give you whatever experience…" Eckhart Tolle. *A New Earth*. Penguin, Michael Joseph Publishers. 2005

Chapter 1: My Early Life

"The initiation of the awakening…" Eckhart Tolle. *A New Earth*. P259. Penguin, Michael Joseph Publishers. 2005

Chapter 3: Guru

"The desire in your mind to meet God…" Shrii Shrii Anandamurti. 1971. From the discourse, *Your Personal Relationship with God*. A'nandavacana'mrtam part 23. AMPS Publications. Electronic Edition 2001, 2006.

"Everything can be taken…" Victor E. Frankl. *Man's Search for Meaning*. Beacon Press. 2006

Chapter 4: Spiritual Teacher

"To cry out to Him…" Anandamayi Ma. Narayan Chaudhuri. *That Compassionate Touch of Ma Anandamayee.* 1980. Motilal Banarsidass Publications. Delhi.

"Once the Guru has accepted…" Anandamayi Ma. Retrieved 2.2.2016 from http://www.anandamayi.org/anandavarta/Vol29No4a.pdf

Chapter 5: A Counsellor

"A compassionate attitude helps…" Dalai Lama. *Compassion makes You Happy.* Retrieved 6.8.2016 from http://www.healyourlife.com/compassion-makes-you-happy

Chapter 6: Communication

Thich Nhat Hanh interviewed by Oprah Winfrey. Retrieved: 12.3.2015. Compassionate Listening.

http://www.supersoul.tv/supersoul-sunday/thich-nhat-hanh-on-compassionate-listening

Chapter 7: Spiritual Coach

"It is but the Self…" Anandamayi Ma. Narayan Chaudhuri. *That Compassionate Touch of Ma Anandamayee.* 1980. Motilal Banarsidass Publications. Delhi.

"Self-knowledge is the true knowledge…" Shrii Shrii Anandamurti. 1971. From the discourse, *What is the Way?* Subha's'ita Sam'graha part 11. AMPS Publications. Electronic Edition 2001, 2006.

Ch. 8 Zhineng Qigong

Shrii Shrii Anandamurti. 1955. *Intuitional Practice and It's Necessity.* Ananda Marga: Elementary Philosophy. AMPA Publications. Electronic Edition 2001,2006

Chapter 9: Intuitive Group

"Is beyond the range of your buddhi… Shrii Shrii Anandamurti. 1979. From the discourse, *The Real Value of the Human Entity,* A'nanda Vacanamrtam part 12. AMPS Publications. Electronic Edition 2001, 2006.

Glossary:

Guru definition: Shrii Shrii Anandamurti. 1978. From the discourse *Guru Puja.* Ananda Vacanamrtam part 3. AMPS Publications. Electronic Edition 2001, 2006.

GOD definition. Shrii Shrii Anandamurti. Date unknown. From the discourse *Pranava.* Ánanda Vacanámrtam Part 34 . AMPS Publications. Electronic Edition 2001, 2006.